Dad Jokes

The Good, The Bad, And The Just Plain Stupid

Printed in the United States of America

First Printing, 2018

ISBN-13: 978-1723539992

ISBN-10: 1723539996

Joshua Shifrin

Shifrinbooks.com

Dad Jokes
The Good, The Bad, And The Just Plain Stupid

-Dedication-

To my fantastic nieces and nephews.
Liyam, Eilat, Samantha, Ethan, Neve, and Reece
I love you – Uncle Josh

Dad Jokes
The Good, The Bad, And The Just Plain Stupid

-Introduction-

I was one of the lucky ones. I grew up with a GREAT dad!
He loves his family, is a hard worker, and best of all he's
really funny! Even as a child, I always knew that someday,
when I had a family of my own, I would aspire to be just
like my father. Well, that day is here.

I'm also blessed to have a terrific wife and two amazing
sons! And while I'm far from perfect, I do my best to be the
type of father that my kids can look up to. I work hard, play
sports with my boys, and even do my best to help them
with their homework when I can (although I have to admit,
as they get older that's becoming increasingly difficult).

And I truly love being a dad. Every part of it. But one of
my favorite 'duties' as a father (yes, I just said "duties") is
making my boys laugh. Although my family thinks I'm as
corny as a field in Iowa, telling a great "Dad Joke" and
seeing my boys try to stifle a laugh, brings me as much joy
as a pig in mud. And for years I've experimented with them
all. The good jokes, the bad ones, and the truly just plain
old stupid — which are my favorites. But why should I
keep all of my hilarious wit to myself? As my parents
always taught me, share the wealth.

Dad Jokes

The Good, The Bad, And The Just Plain Stupid

So I've put together some of the best tried-and-true dad jokes that are sure to get a chuckle. Maybe your kids might not laugh overtly, but somewhere, deep inside, they'll be snickering … whether it be *with* you or *at* you, I can't say for sure. But as a dad, I've learned that sometimes you need to take what your kids are willing to offer.

So I hope you enjoy ***Dad Jokes: The Good, The Bad, And The Just Plain Stupid*** half as much as I do. And whether your children end up laughing, or simply rolling their eyes at your ineptness, you'll have the satisfaction of carrying out the centuries-old tradition of doing what dads do best: being there for your family, loving them, caring for them, and every once in a while even making them laugh.

To dads everywhere — this book is for you!

Dad Jokes

The Good, The Bad, And The Just Plain Stupid

A father tomato was out for a walk with his son. The inquisitive boy tomato was constantly stopping to look at the things that he found interesting. It was getting late, and the dad was starting to get upset. He continuously prompted his son to pick up the pace, but the boy continued to lag behind. Finally, the exasperated father lifted up his foot, smashed it down on top of the little tomato, and yelled, "Ketchup!!"

Dad Jokes
The Good, The Bad, And The Just Plain Stupid

Why can't you trust atoms?
They make up everything.

What do you call cheese that belongs to someone else?
Nacho Cheese.

How many psychologists does it take to change a light bulb?
Only one but the light bulb has to really want to change.

Why did the bicycle continue to fall over?
It was two tired.

How does a duck pay for her lip gloss?
She simply puts it on her bill.

What did the hat say to the shirt?
You stay here, I'll go on ahead.

Dad Jokes
The Good, The Bad, And The Just Plain Stupid

How do you become best friends with a squirrel?

Just act like a nut.

Why did the man get fired from the calendar factory?

Because he took a few days off.

Dad Jokes
The Good, The Bad, And The Just Plain Stupid

**I'm reading a great book about
anti-gravity.**
I can't put it down.

**I bought a thesaurus but when I opened
it up, I noticed all of the pages were
blank.**
*I have no words to describe how upset I
am.*

Dad Jokes
The Good, The Bad, And The Just Plain Stupid

Did You Know?

Father's Day was founded by Sonora Smart Dodd at the YMCA in Spokane, Washington in 1910. Dodd, who was born in Arkansas, planned the celebration held on June 19 that first year. Dodd's father was a Civil War veteran named William Jackson Smart. He was a single parent who raised his six children.

What do you call a cow in a tornado?
A milkshake.

What type of fish is sure to end up in heaven?
An angelfish.

Dad Jokes
The Good, The Bad, And The Just Plain Stupid

What is the difference between being ignorant and being apathetic?
I don't know and I don't care.

Why is England such a wet country?
Because the Queen reigns there.

Dad Jokes
The Good, The Bad, And The Just Plain Stupid

**What did the buffalo say to his son
when he went off to college?**

Bison.

**Did you hear about the new restaurant
on the moon?**

Great food but no atmosphere.

Dad Jokes
The Good, The Bad, And The Just Plain Stupid

How did the nun make holy water?
She boiled the hell out of it.

How in the world do parents lose their kids?
Seriously, any advice would be appreciated.

There is a new show about beavers.
It is the best dam program I've even seen.

What type of frog can jump higher than a house?
All of them ... houses can't jump.

Dad Jokes

The Good, The Bad, And The Just Plain Stupid

A mushroom was out walking on a warm day. After a while he became thirsty and found a neighborhood watering hole. He walked into the bar, found a seat, and ordered a beer. The bartender took one look at him and said, "I'm sorry, we don't serve mushrooms here." The mushroom simply laughed and said, "Why not? I'm a fun-guy."

Did you know that math is a difficult subject?
It's been proven that 5/4 of people struggle with fractions.

What can you serve but never eat?
A tennis ball.

Dad Jokes
The Good, The Bad, And The Just Plain Stupid

What is a cow's favorite thing to read?
A Cattle-log.

Why do the phone companies try to hire employees from the hospital?
There are a lot of good operators there.

What do you call an elephant that no one cares about?

An irrelephant.

Do you know why the invisible man turned down a high-paying job?

He just couldn't see himself doing it.

Dad Jokes
The Good, The Bad, And The Just Plain Stupid

**What's easy for kids to get into, but
hard for them to get out of?**
Trouble.

Where do Eskimos keep their money?
In snow banks.

How much does a pirate pay for corn?
A buccaneer.

Why is it hard for Russian dolls to make friends?
They're completely full of themselves.

Dad Jokes

The Good, The Bad, And The Just Plain Stupid

Did You Know?

British scientist Bertold Wiesner reportedly fathered approximately 1,000 children through artificial insemination by donating sperm at his own London fertility clinic in the 1940s.

Dad Jokes
The Good, The Bad, And The Just Plain Stupid

A man walked into a bar.
The next man ducked.

Why were the elephants banned from the pool?
They kept dropping their trunks.

Dad Jokes
The Good, The Bad, And The Just Plain Stupid

What country has the best sprinters?
The Russians.

If you need to move, what type of citizen would be the most helpful?
A Pakistani.

How do you know if you've been to an emotional wedding?
Even the cake will be in tiers.

Why can't T-Rexes clap their hands?
Because they're extinct.

Why did the jury decide that the picture was innocent?

Because it was framed.

What is the best time to go to the dentist?

Tooth Hurt-y.

Why are stadiums so hot in the off season?

Because there are no fans in them.

Why do dads tell the worst jokes?

Because we're Groan-ups.

Dad Jokes
The Good, The Bad, And The Just Plain Stupid

My grandfather warned people over and over that the Titanic would sink. He kept warning them but they wouldn't listen. He even started to yell at the top of his lungs that the Titanic would go down. Eventually they got sick of him and kicked him out of the theatre.

Dad Jokes
The Good, The Bad, And The Just Plain Stupid

Did you hear about the tough chef who claimed the only food that could make him cry was an onion?
I hit him in the head with a coconut.

Why did the entrepreneur sheep go out of business?
Because he was full of baaaaaaaaad ideas.

Dad Jokes
The Good, The Bad, And The Just Plain Stupid

Did you hear the joke about the roof?
Never mind ... it's over your head.

Did you hear the joke about the broken pencil?
Never mind ... it's pointless.

What did the reassuring blanket say to the bed?

I've got you covered.

I've had the recurring dream that I'm a car muffler.

Now I'm exhausted.

Dad Jokes
The Good, The Bad, And The Just Plain Stupid

**Don't ever buy anything with
Velcro...**
It's a rip-off.

Why are frogs unable to fix computers?
*Because they always end up with too many
bugs.*

Dad Jokes
The Good, The Bad, And The Just Plain Stupid

Why do skunks make such good judges?
They bring odor to the court.

Why did the librarian miss her flight?
Because it was overbooked.

Dad Jokes
The Good, The Bad, And The Just Plain Stupid

<u>Did You Know?</u>

According to Salon *magazine, the top 10 worst movie dads of all-time are:*

1) *John Milton, The Devil's Advocate*
2) *Darth Vader, Star Wars*
3) *Noah Cross, Chinatown*
4) *Grandpa, The Texas Chainsaw Massacre*
5) *The Rev. Harry Powell, aka Preacher, Night of the Hunter*
6) *Jack Torrance, The Shining*
7) *Brad Whitewood Sr., At Close Range*
8) *Bill Maplewood, Happiness*
9) *Ed Wilson, Natural Born Killers*
10) *Dwight Hansen, This Boy's Life*

Dad Jokes
The Good, The Bad, And The Just Plain Stupid

What did the peanut farmer say to his good-for-nothing son?
You're driving me nuts.

"Hey, Dad, do you know where my sunglasses are?"
"They're right next to my dad glasses."

Dad Jokes
The Good, The Bad, And The Just Plain Stupid

What does a good spy always wear?
Sneakers.

What is the best season to jump on a trampoline?
Spring time.

Waiter: "Do you wanna box for your leftover food?"
Customer: "No thanks, but I'll wrestle you for them."

Why do so many plumbers retire early?
Their work is draining.

Dad Jokes
The Good, The Bad, And The Just Plain Stupid

**What do you call a dog that loves
playing in the snow?**
A chilly dog.

**Why was the cat banned from
the casino?**
It turns out he was a cheetah.

Why did the peanut have to go to the police station?

He was a-salted.

Why did the coffee have to go to the same police station?

It got mugged.

Dad Jokes

The Good, The Bad, And The Just Plain Stupid

A teenager told his father that he was having trouble with his dad's car. "What's the problem?" the man asked. "The carburetor has water in it" replied the son. "That doesn't make any sense" the father retorted. But the son insisted that he was sure that the carburetor had water in it. After going around in circles, the dad became increasingly frustrated. Finally, the father got out of his comfortable chair and said, "Let me see the car." He went to the garage but it wasn't there. "Where in the world is my car?!" the exasperated man asked. The son looked his father directly in the shoes and responded, "In the pool."

Why didn't the teddy bear want dessert?
Because he was stuffed.

What do you call bears with no ears?
B.

Dad Jokes
The Good, The Bad, And The Just Plain Stupid

Did you hear about the new peanut?
It's nuts.

What do you call a person with no body and no nose?
Nobody knows.

Dad Jokes
The Good, The Bad, And The Just Plain Stupid

I was going to tell you a joke about a high jump.
But never mind...I'm over it.

Do you know why you can't hear a pterodactyl go to the bathroom?
Because the pee is silent.

Dad Jokes
The Good, The Bad, And The Just Plain Stupid

Why did the omelet flunk out of school?
He failed his egg-zams.

Did you hear about the chicken that won the 100-meter freestyle at the Olympics?
He was an egg-cellent swimmer.

What did the egg say in the crowded store?

Egg-scuse me.

How do chickens root for their favorite sports team?

They 'egg' them on.

<u>Did You Know?</u>

While no one knows for sure where the word 'Dad' originated, it is widely believed that it came from baby talk when young children would babble with 'dada.'

Dad Jokes
The Good, The Bad, And The Just Plain Stupid

**What did the father chimney say
to his son?**

You're too young to smoke.

Why are frogs always so happy?

They simply eat whatever bugs them.

Dad Jokes
The Good, The Bad, And The Just Plain Stupid

**Did you hear about the two satellites
that got married?**
*The wedding wasn't that impressive but
the reception was incredible.*

**What the most famous animal
in the sea?**
The starfish.

Dad Jokes
The Good, The Bad, And The Just Plain Stupid

**What do you get when you cross a loaf
of bread with a bunch of lemons?**
Sourdough.

**Why is the fog constantly
in the hospital?**
Because it's always under the weather.

Dad Jokes
The Good, The Bad, And The Just Plain Stupid

**Do you know why cemeteries are
so popular?**
People are dying to get in.

**Did you ever hear the joke about a piece
of paper?**
Never mind, it's tearable.

Do you know what to do if you see an envelope on fire?

Stamp it out.

How many pencils can be put into an empty pencil case?

Just one. After that it won't be empty anymore.

Dad Jokes
The Good, The Bad, And The Just Plain Stupid

In math class, a teacher asked her students who could answer the following question: "If I gave you two dogs, then two more, and then another two, how many dogs would you have?" Little Johnny in the front row raised his hand and answered "Seven." "That's close," the teacher said. She repeated the question but Johnny still responded with "Seven." The teacher then said, "Listen carefully. What is $2 + 2 + 2$ and Johnny answered with "Six." "So if you know how to do the problem," the exasperated teacher retorted "Why do you keep answering with 'seven'?" "Because I already own a dog."

Dad Jokes
The Good, The Bad, And The Just Plain Stupid

Why are famous people so cool?
They get a lot of fan mail.

Why are oak trees often so unpopular?
They throw off a lot of shade.

Dad Jokes
The Good, The Bad, And The Just Plain Stupid

I told my girlfriend to meet me at the gym but then I didn't go.
I hope she understands that we're not working out.

What did the man say to the lightning bolt at his surprise party?
You really shocked me.

Did you hear about the gardener on the first day of spring?

She was so excited that she wet her plants.

Dad: "Why didn't you tell me that you just ate a tube full of glue?"

Child: "My lips were sealed."

Dad Jokes
The Good, The Bad, And The Just Plain Stupid

Why don't mothers of basketball players wear big earrings?

Because they're tired of all the hoops.

What's the best part about living in Switzerland?

Well, the flag is a big plus.

Dad Jokes
The Good, The Bad, And The Just Plain Stupid

What soda do cheerleaders love to drink?

Root beer.

Why are so many math teachers overweight?

They love pi.

Dad Jokes

The Good, The Bad, And The Just Plain Stupid

Did You Know?

One of the funniest dads on the planet, Eddie Murphy, has nine children. One can only assume that his 'Dad Jokes' are some of the best.

Did you hear about the famous shrink who wrote a book on reverse psychology?
It's called, Don't Read This Book.

A roast beef sandwich walks into a bar and orders a beer.
The bartender says, "Sorry, we don't serve food here."

Dad Jokes
The Good, The Bad, And The Just Plain Stupid

What did the salesmen say to the professor after he put on a suit?
You're looking smart.

What did the chef say to the knife?
You're looking sharp.

How do meteorologists always make a little extra money?
They're the first to know about any change in the weather.

What is a wizard's favorite food?
Sandwitches.

Dad Jokes
The Good, The Bad, And The Just Plain Stupid

Why didn't the saxophone player get picked to play in the band?
He blew his audition.

What did the thermometer say to the cute thermometer next to him?
You make my temperature rise.

Why did the thermometer have to go to the doctor in Florida?

Because he had a high temperature.

Why did the vampire need to go to the doctor?

He couldn't stop coffin.

Dad Jokes

The Good, The Bad, And The Just Plain Stupid

"I know a man who is 100 years old and works out every day," a father told his son. "That's incredible," the son replied. "What does he do?" "He gets up at the crack of dawn and runs two miles." "Wow" the son said. "What does he do in the afternoon?" The father smiled and said, "The second mile."

**Why did the computer need to go to
the doctor?**
Because it had a virus.

**Why did the bird need to go to
the doctor?**
He needed a 'Tweet-ment.'

Dad Jokes
The Good, The Bad, And The Just Plain Stupid

Why did the banana need to go to the doctor?
Because it was not peeling well.

What do you call a snowman in the middle of the summer?
A puddle.

Dad Jokes
The Good, The Bad, And The Just Plain Stupid

How do you make a tissue dance?
Put a little boogie in it.

Why didn't the crab have any friends?
Because he was shellfish.

Dad Jokes
The Good, The Bad, And The Just Plain Stupid

Why do birds fly south for the winter?
They don't know how to drive.

**How do you know if an ant is male
or female?**
*Of course they're female, otherwise they'd
be uncles.*

Why was the failing student so wet?
Because he was below 'C' level.

**Why are belts always getting into
trouble with the law?**
They're constantly holding up pants.

Dad Jokes
The Good, The Bad, And The Just Plain Stupid

<u>Did You Know?</u>

While many countries celebrate Father's Day, it is celebrated at different times around the world. Australia and New Zealand honor fathers on the first Sunday in September; Spain and Belgium celebrate them on March 19; and in Canada, Britain, and the U.S., Father's Day is celebrated on the third Sunday in June.

Dad Jokes
The Good, The Bad, And The Just Plain Stupid

What did the triangle say to the circle?
You're pointless.

What did the dime say to the quarter?
We just make cents together.

Dad Jokes
The Good, The Bad, And The Just Plain Stupid

**Why did the frog need to take a bus
to work?**
Because his car got toad.

**Where is a worm's favorite place
to vacation?**
The Big Apple.

What type of phone should you use at the ocean?

A shell-phone.

What did a pharaoh do when he was afraid?

Talked to his mummy.

Dad Jokes
The Good, The Bad, And The Just Plain Stupid

Did you hear about the man who stole a cheese sandwich?
The police really grilled him.

Why did the yogurt go to the symphony?
Because it was cultured.

Why was the doctor getting frustrated?
Because he was losing his patients.

Why can't a nose be 12 inches long?
Because then it would be a foot.

Dad Jokes

The Good, The Bad, And The Just Plain Stupid

There were once a pair of brothers named 'Mind Your Own Business' and 'Trouble.' One day they decided to play hide and seek. Trouble went to hide and Mind Your Own Business began to look for him. He looked everywhere but couldn't find him. Eventually, a police officer noticed Mind Your Own Business looking into a garbage can behind a local store. "What is your name?" asked the officer. "Mind Your Own Business," replied the boy. The officer, now angry, stated, "Are you looking for trouble?" Mind Your Own Business smiled and said, "Why yes … yes I am."

Dad Jokes
The Good, The Bad, And The Just Plain Stupid

**Why is it hard to surprise Darth Vader
with a gift for his birthday?**

Because he could sense your presents.

**Why did the thermometer drop out
of school?**

Because he already had multiple degrees.

Dad Jokes
The Good, The Bad, And The Just Plain Stupid

Did you know that French Fries aren't cooked in France?
They're cooked in Greece.

Why did the sesame seed win so much money at the casino?
Because he was on a roll.

**I'm the most motivating employee
at work.**
*Everyone says they work twice as hard
when I'm around.*

Why was the nectarine so popular?
*All of his friends thought he was
a real peach.*

Dad Jokes
The Good, The Bad, And The Just Plain Stupid

What do you call a cow with two legs?
Lean Beef.

What do you call a cow with no legs?
Ground Beef.

What did the sink say to the toilet?
You look flushed.

What did the salad say to the man at the refrigerator?
Close the door, I'm dressing.

Dad Jokes
The Good, The Bad, And The Just Plain Stupid

Did You Know?

Actor Charlie Sheen has one of the largest child support payments in Hollywood. Sheen has two baby-mamas, each with two of his kids. Sheen pays his ex-wives, Denise Richards and Brooke Mueller, $55,000 per month each for a grand total of $110,000 per month or $1.32 million per year.

What did the traffic light say to the driver?

Look away ... I'm changing.

Why did the traffic light turn red?

You would be embarrassed too if you had to change in the middle of the street.

Dad Jokes
The Good, The Bad, And The Just Plain Stupid

**Do you want to hear a good joke
about pizza?**
Never mind ... it's cheesy.

Why do cows like astronomy?
The enjoy looking at the moooooooon.

Where do cows like to hang their paintings?
In the moooo-seum.

I only know 25 English letters.
I don't know why.

Dad Jokes
The Good, The Bad, And The Just Plain Stupid

Why was 6 afraid of 7?
Because 7, 8, 9.

Why are fish so smart?
They hang out in schools.

What do dads love to eat at the movies?
Pop-corn.

Why did the boy throw the clock out of his window?
Because he wanted to see time fly.

Dad Jokes

The Good, The Bad, And The Just Plain Stupid

A man went to his priest to talk about his final wishes. "I'd like to be cremated," the man said. "And then I'd like my ashes sprinkled all over my wife's favorite clothing store." The priest looked surprised and said, "Why would you want your ashes put there?" "That way," the man said, "my wife will be sure to visit me every day."

Dad Jokes
The Good, The Bad, And The Just Plain Stupid

What is the most expensive fish?
Goldfish.

Why did the bird get kicked out of the soccer game?
For fowl play.

Dad Jokes
The Good, The Bad, And The Just Plain Stupid

What is green and smells like red paint?
Green paint.

**What did the teenager say when he was
fired from the rubber band factory?**
Oh, snap!

How did the hairdresser win the race?
She took a shortcut.

**What vegetable should you always eat
with a doctor near you?**
An artichoke.

Dad Jokes
The Good, The Bad, And The Just Plain Stupid

Why did the ghost decide to skip the dance?
Because he had no-body to go with.

Why was the baby strawberry crying?
Because his parents were in a jam.

**Why do most people avoid eating
clown fishes?**
They taste a little funny.

**Who did Exxon call when they had an
oil spill in the ocean?**
A mermaid.

Did You Know?

Historically, dads were often deferred from the draft during America's wars. Single men were drafted first.

Why was the shirt heartbroken?
*Because he was in glove with a sock but
she shooed him away.*

Why are bakers so rich?
Because they raise so much dough.

**What is an astronaut's favorite key on
a computer?**
The space bar.

**Did you hear about the puddle that
bombed at the comedy show?**
He was all dried up.

Dad Jokes
The Good, The Bad, And The Just Plain Stupid

Why are skeletons such scaredy-cats?
They don't have any guts.

How do you know if a ghost is lying?
You can see right through them.

Dad Jokes
The Good, The Bad, And The Just Plain Stupid

**Did you hear about the three year old
who fell off a ladder and didn't
get hurt?**
She fell off the bottom step.

**Why did the man put $100 in
the freezer?**
Because he wanted cold, hard cash.

Dad Jokes
The Good, The Bad, And The Just Plain Stupid

Why did the man need to go out with a prune?
Because he couldn't find a date.

Why did the koala leave his mate?
He couldn't bear it any longer.

Dad Jokes
The Good, The Bad, And The Just Plain Stupid

A man was applying to be an officer in the Army but was getting the runaround. The exasperated candidate pleaded his case. "I have a genius IQ, I received a perfect score on my SATs, and I was number one in my class at a prestigious university. So what's the problem?" "You don't seem to understand," said the Captain. "Intelligence is not a requirement in the military."

Why wasn't the polygon very popular?
He was too square.

**How do you know when grapes
are tired?**
They'll start to wine.

What is a light year?
It's similar to a regular year but only with fewer calories.

Why was the music conference so bad?
Because the speakers were awful.

Do you know the worst part about hugging the most attractive person I know?

Smacking into the mirror.

What kind of key can not only open a banana, but can also eat it?

A monkey.

Dad Jokes
The Good, The Bad, And The Just Plain Stupid

What is the best day to go to the beach?
Sun-day.

**What word is spelled incorrectly in
every English dictionary around
the world?**
'Wrong.'

Dad Jokes
The Good, The Bad, And The Just Plain Stupid

Why do fish live in salt water?
Because they hate pepper.

Why did the cookie end up in the hospital?
Because it felt crummy.

Dad Jokes
The Good, The Bad, And The Just Plain Stupid

<u>Did You Know?</u>

MensFitness.com asked 100 women their thoughts about dating men with 'Dad Bods.' While 50% of the women were indifferent and 38% stated that they wanted their men in top shape, a surprising 15% of women said they exclusively date men with a Dad Bod.

Dad Jokes
The Good, The Bad, And The Just Plain Stupid

**What starts with a 'P', ends with an 'E',
and has thousands of letters in it?**
Post Office.

Who was the best lawyer at the firm?
Sue, of course.

Dad Jokes
The Good, The Bad, And The Just Plain Stupid

Why are chickens so musical?

Because they have their own drumsticks.

What's black and white and red all over?

A newspaper.

What else is black and white and red all over?

A skunk with a sunburn.

What's brown and sticky?

A stick.

Dad Jokes
The Good, The Bad, And The Just Plain Stupid

What did one wall say to the other wall?
I'll meet you at the corner.

What has four wheels and flies?
A garbage truck.

**Why did the mom and dad grapes really
need a vacation?**
*They were exhausted from raisin
their kids.*

What is the saddest tree?
A weeping willow.

Dad Jokes

The Good, The Bad, And The Just Plain Stupid

I once knew a man who had a lot of problems. For one, he was dyslexic. Secondly, he was agnostic. And lastly, he suffered from insomnia. The poor guy used to stay up all night wondering if there really was a dog.

Dad Jokes
The Good, The Bad, And The Just Plain Stupid

Why do people like banana milkshakes?
They have appeal.

**Where did the snowman find
his princess?**
At the snowball.

Why did the orange juice fail out of school?

Due to a lack of concentration.

Why did the golfer throw away his shoes?

There was a hole in one.

Dad Jokes
The Good, The Bad, And The Just Plain Stupid

"Dad, can you put my shoes on?"
"No, son, they won't fit me."

What did the zero say to the eight?
Nice belt.

Dad Jokes
The Good, The Bad, And The Just Plain Stupid

How do oceans say hello to you?
They wave.

What is the best way to catch a school of fish?
With bookworms.

Why can't pigs be trusted?
Because they always squeal.

People used to laugh when I told them I was going to write a really funny dad joke book.
Well, no one is laughing now.

Did You Know?

While nobody knows for sure, it is believed that the world's oldest father is Ramajit Raghav from India. He was 96 years old in 2010 when his 52-year-old wife gave birth to a baby boy. Raghav was a bachelor until he was in his 80s

48078077R00066

Made in the USA
Middletown, DE
12 June 2019